I Love Poems!

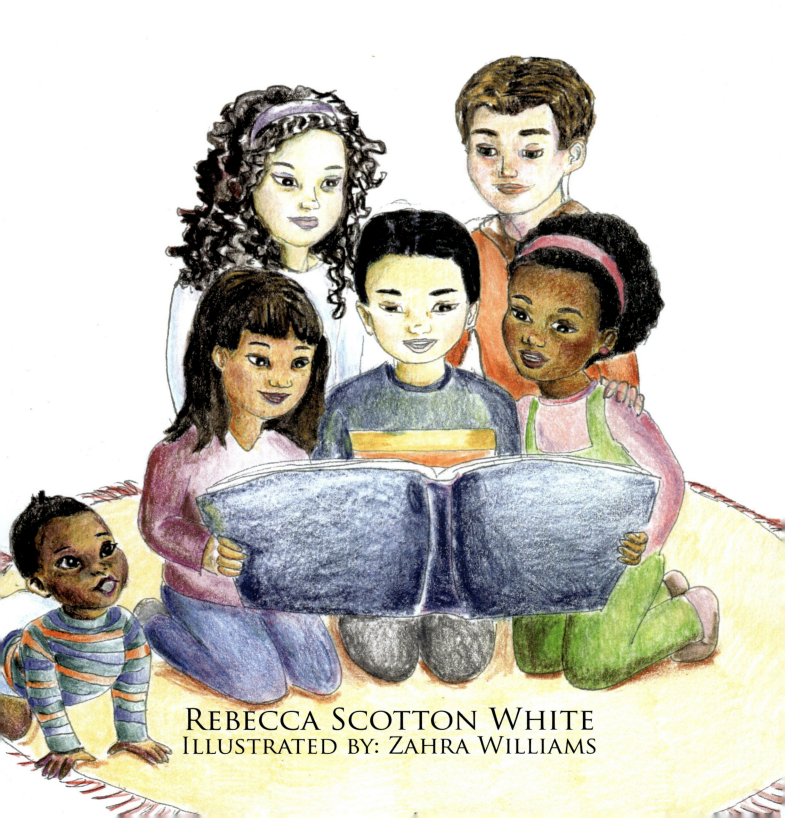

Rebecca Scotton White
Illustrated by: Zahra Williams

Print information available on the last page

Rev. date: 11/13/2019

To order additional copies of this book, contact:
Xlibris
1-888-795-4274
www.Xlibris.com
Orders@Xlibris.com

Dedication:

To my grandchildren,
Bryanna, Jaden, Justin, Little Baby AJ,
The Scotton and White families, and other relatives

Acknowlegements:

To my sister, Gail and my nephew, Matthew,
Thanks for giving me the thu mbs up for my first poetry book.

To my niece, Zahra,
Thank you for the beautiful illustrations.

To my sister Gwen,
Thanks for the excellent editing.

Love you all!

Credits:
Author: Rebecca Scotton White
Cover Illustrations : Zahra Williams
Inside Illustrations: Zahra Williams
Editor: Dr. Gwendolyn Scotton Bethea

This Little Baby

This little baby likes to eat, eat, eat.

This little baby likes to dance on his feet.

This little baby likes to play, play, play.

This little baby likes to crawl away.

This little baby likes to cry all day long.

This little baby likes to hear happy songs.

6

Nap Time

Come to mama little baby.

It's time for a nap.

Come to mama little baby.

Get into my lap.

Come to mama little baby.

Now, don't make a peep.

Come to mama little baby.

It's time to go to sleep!

My Special Teddy Bear

Jaden, it's time for bed.

Are you ready?

Not yet mom,

I've lost my teddy.

I love my fuzzy brown teddy bear.

He's very special to me!

Sometimes he likes to play hide and seek.

Now, where can my teddy bear be?

I've looked in places

High and low.

Where oh where

Did my teddy bear go?

Please come out

Wherever you are!

I know my teddy bear

Cannot be far!

There you are, teddy bear.

I've looked all day!

I'm glad I've found you.

Now in my arms, you'll stay!

Goodnight, teddy bear,

Don't you try again to run away!

Sleepy Bear

Winter is coming!

Are you sleepy little bear?

Your warm den is waiting

For you, over there!

Don't forget to eat

And get fat, fat, fat.

You won't have to eat for months.

Now what do you think of that?

Eat, hungry little bear.

Don't worry about the pounds.

There might be snow during the winter.

Very little food will be found!

Go to sleep little bear,

You tiny little thing.

When you wake up.

It will be spring!

This Little Black Cub

This little black cub eats honey.

This little black cub eats fish.

This little black cub is funny.

This little black cub eats from a dish.

This little black cub looks at the stars

And makes a special wish!

The Crickets' Happy Little Song

Early one morning, before the break of day,

Two little crickets came out to sing and play.

"Be quiet!" I said. "Please, if you will!"

But, they were so happy and couldn't keep still.

"You will be sorry, if I get up from my bed!"

They just laughed at me and shook their heads.

They were dancing, jumping, hopping along,

Shouting and singing this happy little song.

I won't look down, down, down and sad, sad, sad.

I'll hold my head up and be glad, glad, glad!

No worries or frowns can get me down.

I'll hop all day and make happy sounds!

Farmer Brown's Farm

The old red rooster says, "cock-a-doodle doo!"

The hungry calf says, "moo, moo!"

The huge black crow says, "caw, caw!"

The sleepy gray donkey says, "hee haw, hee haw!"

The tiny white lamb says, "baa, baa!"

16

The little kid goat says, "maa, maa!"

The muddy pink piglet says, "oink, oink!"

The noisy baby gosling says, "honk, honk!"

The galloping black colt says, "neigh, neigh!"

Famer Brown says, "okay, okay!"

The Baby Ducklings

The baby ducklings like to sing, quack, and play.

They like to swim in the cool water all day.

Splash, splash, splash all day long,

Singing and quacking silly little songs.

Mr. Cat

Mr. Cat, Mr. Cat

So furry,

Where are you going in such a hurry?

Are you looking for the little mouse?

Too late! He's already in his little house!

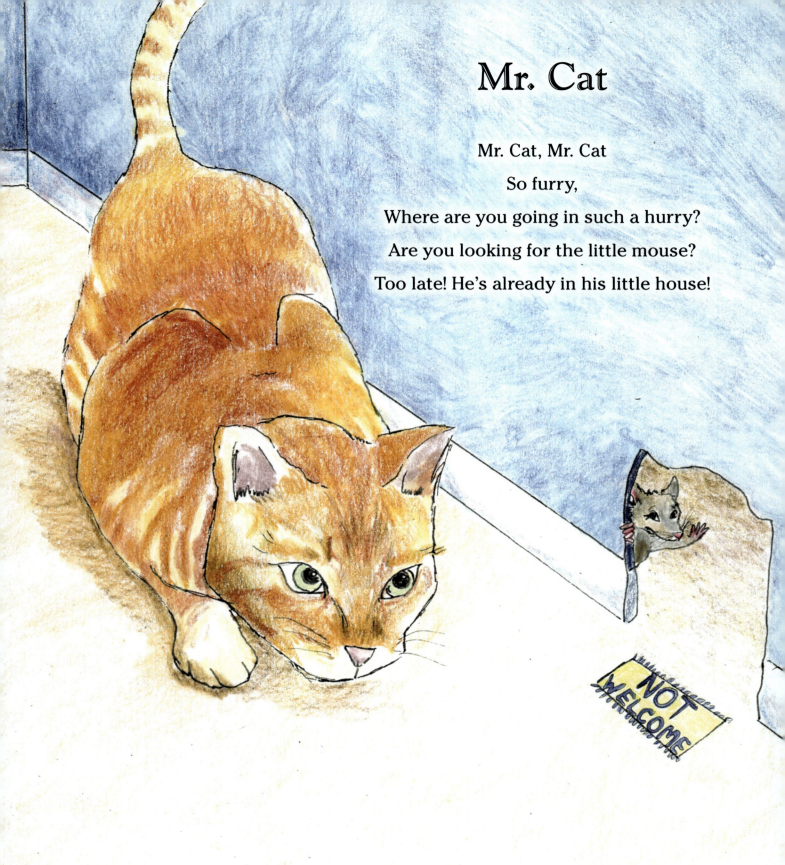

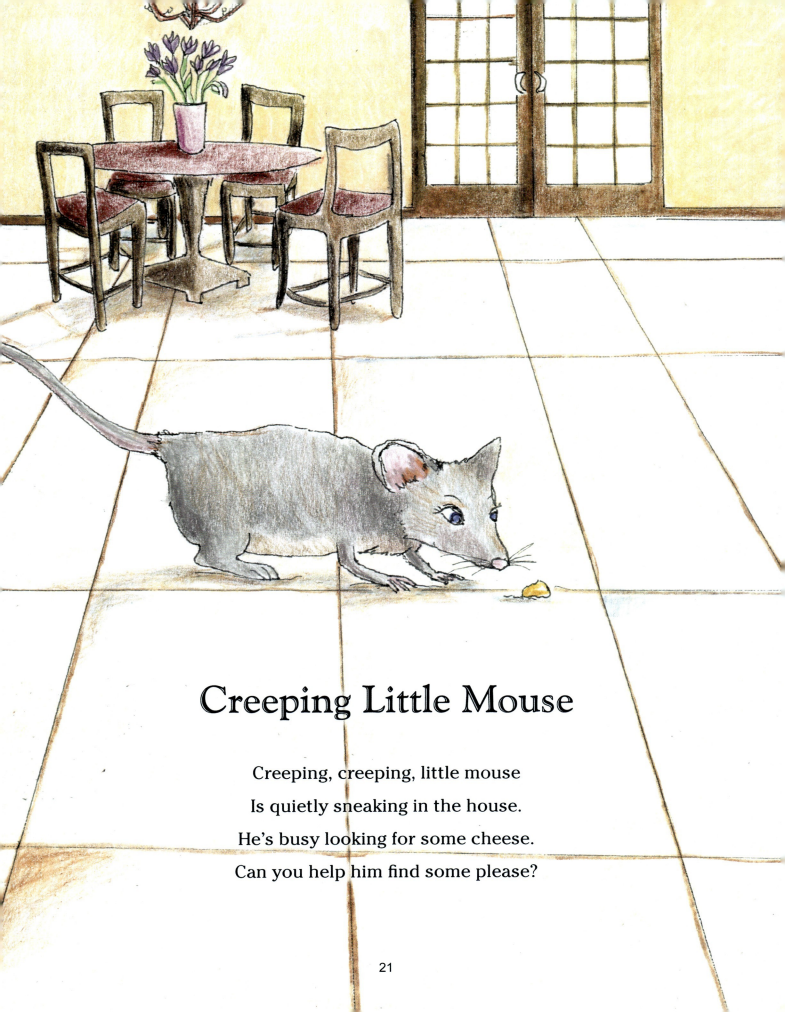

Creeping Little Mouse

Creeping, creeping, little mouse

Is quietly sneaking in the house.

He's busy looking for some cheese.

Can you help him find some please?

A Wonderful Surprise!

A tiny gray mouse was searching for cheese,

Slowly creeping around the house one day.

He suddenly let out an enormous sneeze, AHH…CHOO!

Mr. Cat came running his way.

"Please, Please, let me go Mr Cat,"

Begged the tiny gray mouse with giant tears in his eyes.

Mr. Cat replied, "Okay, I'll do that."

Oh, what a wonderful surprise!

I'm Flying!

A baby bird fell from his tree.

He cried, "Please, please, help me!

I haven't yet learned how to fly!"

The mama bird came swooping by.

She suddenly caught the tiny little thing.

She said, "All you have to do is flap your wings.

Believe in yourself and try, try, try!"

"I'm flying! I'm flying! What a smart little bird am I!"

Little Hungry Birdies

Little hungry birdies,

Going tweet, tweet, tweet.

Singing for their supper,

Ready to eat, eat, eat.

Hurry back, mama bird!

We've been singing all day.

Waiting for you to bring

Delicious worms our way.

Fat ones, skinny ones, bring all kinds.

We really don't care!

Bring all you can find!

I'm back baby birdies

With worms for your tummies.

Thank you, mama bird.

They are so yummy!

The Beach

I like to go to the beach a lot!

The sun at the beach is so very hot!

I like to cool off by splashing in the ocean.

But I can't forget my sunscreen lotion.

If I do, I will soon learn… OUCH!

My skin will get an awful burn.

I like to drink ice, cold lemonade,

While resting under the umbrella in the shade.

I like to play in the cool grainy sand.

I like the way it feels on my toes and hands.

I like to go exploring for all kinds of seashells.

I'll gather them up and put them in my pail.

I like to see the bright colors in the setting sun.

Watching the beautiful sunrise is so much fun!

It's time again to swim and play,

At the beach on this hot summer day!

Autumn Leaves

Autumn is here!

Look at the colorful leaves.

The leaves are dancing

On the trees!

They are beautiful colors,

Yellow, red, orange, and brown.

Now, the strong wind

Is blowing them down,

Down, down, and all around.

The leaves are falling

Without making a sound.

Mr. Turkey

"Gobble, gobble," says Mr. Turkey.

"You can't catch me!"

Wobble, wobble goes Mr. Turkey,

Running around the oak tree.

"I won't be coming for dinner,

No way! No way!

I'm going out of town

On Thanksgiving Day!"

SANTA

Hey, boys and girls,

Santa's on his way!

Hey, boys and girls,

Santa has toys in his sleigh.

Close your eyes and do not peep.

You'd better hurry and go to sleep.

Santa's headed to your house today,

Hurray!

Zoo Animals

The monkey likes to play, run, and hide.

The elephant likes to swing his trunk from side to side.

The flamingo likes to stand with one foot on the ground.

The lion likes to make a growling sound.

38

Shoes, Shoes, Shoes!

Ice skating shoes are for sliding.

Rollerblading shoes are for gliding.

Sunday dress shoes are shiny.

Little baby shoes are tiny.

Beach shoes are called flip-flops.

Funny clown shoes have pointed tops.

Rain shoes are good for jumping into puddles.

Spiked shoes are for football huddles.

Bedroom shoes are fluffy and soft.

Some shoes are made out of leather or cloth.

Ballet shoes are great for dancing.

Horses' shoes are nice for prancing.

Hats, Hats, Hats!

Hats with tiny leopard spots

Hats with huge polka dots

Baseball hats for wearing to games

Dainty hats for little dames

Cowboy hats wide and tall

Clown hats so silly—some big, some small

Hats with pretty satin bows

Others so floppy and hanging so low

Hats on policemen patrolling the streets

Hats on firemen braving the heat

Patriotic hats—red white and blue

Hats for me and hats for you

More Hats!

Some hats are striped and plaid.

Some hats are made for lassies and lads.

Sun visors keep the sun from your eyes.

Chefs wear hats when baking cookies, cakes, and pies.

Safari hats are good when going on hikes.

Helmets are used when riding bikes.

Straw hats are worn when tanning in the sun.

Party hats are worn just for fun.

There are cute little bonnets for crying babies.

And fancy hats with feathers for ladies.

Rain hats keep us nice and dry.

Which ones would you like to buy?

Printed in the United States
By Bookmasters